THE AMAZING BIBLE ADVENTURE FOR KIDS

JOSH McDOWELL
KEVIN JOHNSON

HARVEST HOUSE PUBLISHERS

EUGENE, OREGON

Cover by Left Coast Design, Portland, Oregon

THE AMAZING BIBLE ADVENTURE FOR KIDS
Copyright © 2006, 2012 by Josh McDowell Ministry and Kevin Johnson
Published by Harvest House Publishers
Eugene, Oregon 97402
www.harvesthousepublishers.com

ISBN 978-0-7369-2877-9 (pbk.)
ISBN 978-0-7369-4229-4 (eBook)

Contents

1

THE WORLD'S GREATEST TREASURE

Your Map to the World's
Most Awesome Treasure: God!

imagine if you heard that a whole bunch of your best friends were coming over any minute to celebrate your birthday—and that each friend was pushing a shopping cart full of presents just for you.

Or suppose someone promised that if you closed your eyes and held out your hands you would get a big surprise—maybe a snuggly new puppy!

Or maybe you received a letter saying that tomorrow your family would fly away on a dream vacation—a month packed with beautiful beaches, thrilling theme parks, and star-packed pro ball games.

How would you react to any one of these nice bits of news?

You would get pretty excited. You probably would jump up and down. Maybe you'd even let loose a squeal of happiness!

But you might get even more noisy and excited if you knew beyond any doubt that there was a vast treasure buried in your yard—a treasure big enough to buy *hundreds* of toy stores or *millions* of puppies or send you and your family on vacation *for the rest of your lives*.

If you knew that your yard held such an awesome treasure, you would run outside and start digging with your bare hands. By day, you would search even in the hot sun or snowy cold. By night, you would light up your work with blazing spotlights.

The Greatest Treasure Ever

You might never experience a totally huge birthday bash...or have a new puppy land in your lap...or fly away on an incredible vacation. And there's not much chance that you will ever find a buried treasure in your yard.

Yet you can find a treasure far bigger and better than anything you can imagine! It's a treasure as real as the book you hold in your hands. It's as near as your next heartbeat. And it's something you don't have to dream about—it can be yours for sure.

This treasure is so totally perfect that it will always supply your most important needs. It will guarantee you more happiness than owning stores stuffed with toys or houses wiggling with puppies. It will offer you a plan for your whole life that is more exciting than a trip around the world.

This treasure isn't just something that makes you giggle and smile for a little while. It makes you happy forever and ever.

Do you want to know what this awesome treasure is? This treasure is *God*.

God is a one-of-a-kind treasure. When you find him, you can live as best friends with the king of the whole universe. He's a friend bigger than a friend. He's the one who can say, "I am the LORD, and there is no other. There is no other God besides me" (Isaiah 45:5 GOD'S WORD). He created the earth and the whole universe. He has the power to calm huge storms and make blind people see. He's the one who cares for our every need. And when Jesus died for our sins, he showed us a love greater than any other.

God's love for you is so enormous that you can spend the rest of your life trying to grasp it. In fact, you can spend all of eternity learning about God's love and living in it—yet there's always more to enjoy! The greatest treasure you can ever possess is having "the power to understand, as all God's people should, how wide, how long, how high, and how deep His love is" (Ephesians 3:18).

The Treasure Map to God's Heart

For every real treasure, there's a map—a piece of paper that tells you exactly how to get to the good stuff.

Here's the amazing part: You probably already have a copy of the treasure map that points you to God. This map that points you straight to him probably sits on your bookshelf or by your bed. The step-by-step directions you need to find the greatest treasure ever are contained in a book that you probably already own. This book is the Bible.

A map won't do you any good if it's parked on your bed stand or stuffed in your back pocket. After all, it's not enough just to have a map. You need to open it up, figure it out, and follow it.

Think about it: If you had a map showing the location of buried jewels and gold, you would work hard to figure out how the map could lead you to that treasure. You would press your nose up close to the map and move your eyes from corner to corner to corner to corner. You would *study* the map. No, not exactly the kind of studying you do at school, but the intense attention you give to things you love and enjoy.

When you poke your nose into God's map, the Bible, and study it, you will come to understand its biggest point—that you can know Jesus as your Savior and friend and enjoy the great life he has planned for you.

It's not enough, however, just to understand what a treasure map shows. You need to be sure the map is real. You don't want to start out following a map scribbled in purple crayon by your little brother or dug out of a box of breakfast cereal. You need to be able to *trust* the map.

It's good to know why you can trust the Bible. In later chapters, we'll look at exactly *why* you can be certain that the Bible is true. You'll see why you can trust the Bible to be the one map that won't lead you on a wild goose chase. You will find that it will truly point you to God.

There's one more thing: A map can't get you to a treasure if you won't move from where you're sitting now. To get to the good stuff, you need to get up and *follow* the map. It's the same with the Bible. You need to know how to put the Bible's instructions into action.

God is the greatest treasure you can ever find, and he's given you a map to get to him—an exciting map that you need to understand, trust, and follow. Do you want to find the really good stuff? Then let's go on a treasure hunt!

2
THE BIG POINT OF GOD'S BIG BOOK

God Put People on Earth to Know Him

f you wanted to draw a map to a treasure that was buried in your backyard, you could probably squeeze it on a tiny scrap of paper. Your directions to find the treasure might be as easy as: "Go out the back door. Take ten steps north and three steps west. Dig."

Figuring out everything that the Bible tells you about God isn't quite that simple. After all, the Bible tells all about how God has gotten along with people from the beginning of the world—and how he will get along with them at the end of time! It gives you huge facts, like how God created the world and what heaven will be like. The front part of the Bible describes how God selected

the Israelites as his chosen people and tells about their struggle to follow him, and the back part teaches us about the birth, death, and life of God's Son, Jesus.

The Bible is so big that if you read one verse a day, you wouldn't finish until you were a very old grandpa or grandma. It would take you more than 85 years to read it all! Even the thinnest Bibles have hundreds and hundreds of pages. If a giant hardcover Bible fell off a shelf onto your head, you could expect a large bump on your noggin.

One Big Message

Yet this big book has a big surprise. Even though the Bible is such a huge book, it contains just one big message. In fact, you can read through the Bible and spot this message as clearly as a line drawn with a fat red marker from the first page to the last. The message is this: *God wants you and everyone else in the world to know him.*

Maybe you already know the big points in the Bible's really long story. It all starts back in the Garden of Eden. God created Adam and Eve and wanted them to be friends with him and with each other. But when those first human beings disobeyed God, their sin hurt the friendship between them and God.

Like Adam and Eve, all of us have sinned and disobeyed God. So all of us have hurt our relationship with God. But God sent his Son, Jesus, to die for our sins and make us friends with him again. God wants all of us to become friends with him now on earth and to live together with him forever in heaven.

That's the big point God wants you to understand: He wants you to know him and be with him forever. Just so that you get this point, there's a verse in the Bible that sums up everything the Bible says. It's as clear as a big X on a treasure map. John 3:16 says, "For God loved the world so much that he gave his one and only Son, so that everyone who believes in him will not perish but have eternal life."

There's no doubt about it. The Bible is a huge book with one message. It's like a perfectly drawn treasure map. It clearly shows the way to the goal.

TREASURE QUEST

Jesus said clearly that eternal life isn't just about living forever. Going to heaven is all about knowing God more and more. Listen to what Jesus taught: "This is eternal life: to know you, the only true God, and Jesus Christ, whom you sent" (John 17:3, GOD'S WORD).

But there's something even more amazing about the Bible: It isn't just one book but a collection of 66 books—39 in the Old Testament and 27 in the New Testament. It was written by more than 40 people, including kings, poor people, fishermen, poets, politicians, and teachers.

Those writers took a whopping 1,500 years to write down all the words in the Bible, yet all their words carry the same message. It's an astonishing sign that the Bible is God's book and that it contains exactly what God wants people to know about him.

FACTOID

The Bible doesn't say exactly how the authors of the Bible knew to write God's words. But 2 Peter 1:21 explains, "No prophecy ever originated from humans. Instead, it was given by the Holy Spirit as humans spoke under God's direction" (GOD'S WORD). The writers of the Bible didn't sit down and draw a map to God all by themselves. The Holy Spirit helped each person write what God wanted and the result is the book we call the Bible—a treasure map to God that has incredibly clear directions.

3

YOU ARE INVITED TO BE GOD'S KID

God Wants You to Know Him

Maybe you have sung the Sunday school song about Zacchaeus—the funny little guy who scooted up a sycamore tree to get a good look at Jesus. The song finishes with a surprise—Jesus points up to Zacchaeus and says, "Come down from that tree right now! Tonight I'm eating supper at *your* house."

Zacchaeus got noticed—by the Son of God!

Most kids would love to get that kind of attention, but few probably expect to have someone famous actually want to meet with them. Maybe you are one of these kids. Maybe you think, *There's nothing special about me. Teachers love kids with brains. Coaches love kids who score lots of points. Choir directors like kids with nice voices. Even naughty kids get noticed by the principal. But me? No one notices me.*

Even if you feel forgotten by everyone else, God knows you're one-of-a-kind special. He not only loves each and every person on planet earth, but he also notices and loves you. He wants to be your friend, just as surely as he made friends with Zacchaeus.

You would be shocked if Jesus drove up to your school, picked you out in a crowd of classmates, and said, "Call your parents! Order a pizza! Tonight I'm coming over to your place for supper!" Yet God thinks you're that special.

When you open the Bible, you'll discover that *you* top the list of all the things God cares about. The Bible says that God "is jealous about his relationship with you" (Exodus 34:14). This kind of jealousy isn't about turning into a green-eyed monster. This kind of jealousy means that God loves you intensely. It's a way to describe how deeply and intensely God cares about his relationship with you. He is completely devoted to you.

God's Eyes Are Totally Glued to You

Exactly how much does God notice about you? He sees everything! He knows you totally! Look what Psalm 139 says:

- God knows where you are at every moment.
- God sees every time you sit down or stand up.
- God knows every thought you think.
- God hears every word before you speak it.

The Bible says that God put you together in your mom's belly. Before you were born, he planned every day of your life. He knows what will happen to you every moment of life. That's amazing!

TRY THIS!

The Bible says that God has counted the hairs on your head. Try using a comb and tweezers to count your hairs one by one—and see how far you get. Beware: By the time you finish that job, you will have grown new hairs and shed a few old ones. God knows everything about you, down to the smallest detail.

3546, 3547, 3548...

God doesn't have a physical body like you do, so you can't see him like he can see you. That's why he gave you the Bible. It's his way of introducing himself to you. Not only is the Bible a map to himself, but it's also a perfect picture of him.

In fact, the Bible shows exactly what God is like. When you read the Bible, you aren't seeing God through an out-of-focus camera. The Bible lets you zoom in close and see that God always loves you, always does right, always tells the truth, and always deserves your trust. And as you read the Bible, there's one truth that is totally clear: God wants you to know him.

TREASURE QUEST

God invites you to be his friend. But it's more than a friendship—it's a relationship so tight that there's only one name for it: *family.* God chose you not just to know him a little bit but also to be his son or daughter. Ephesians 1:4-6 says, "Before the creation of the world, he chose us through Christ to be holy and perfect in his presence. Because of his love he had already decided to adopt us through Jesus Christ. He freely chose to do this so that the kindness he had given us in his dear Son would be praised and given glory" (GOD'S WORD).

God notices you. He calls you his friend. When you trust in Jesus, you become God's son or daughter. You're his child. And that makes God totally happy!

4

THE COOLEST THING YOU CAN EVER BE

God Wants You to Look Like Him

Picture yourself taking a video camera and microphone around your neighborhood, pretending to be a reporter. You could poke the camera in your friends' faces and ask a simple question: "What do you want to be when you grow up?" You would hear all kinds of cool ideas. One kid wants to be a pro basketball player and another wants to be a gymnast. One wants to be an actress and someone else a wildly famous singer.

Those are gigantic dreams. Some people's big dreams do come true. But did you know that God has something even better planned for you? It's the coolest thing you can ever be! Let's see what it is.

Born to Look Like Jesus

God wants you to know him totally, but knowing him is only half of his great plan for you. He also wants you to *be like him*. That's his plan for you and all Christians. The Bible says, "God knew his people in advance, and he chose them to become like his Son" (Romans 8:29). God didn't just think up his plan a few minutes ago. It was his goal from the very beginning!

You probably know families where the brothers and sisters look like miniature versions of their parents. (Maybe that's you!) Most kids look quite a bit like their dad or mom. Just as a father and mother pass their looks and other features down to their children, God made you to look like his Son, Jesus.

Looking like Jesus doesn't mean you sprout a beard, grow out your hair, and go buy a closet full of robes and sandals. It means you become like Jesus in the most important way of all. You start to look like Jesus in everything you think, everything you say, and everything you do. You treat people kindly, just as Jesus did. You speak honestly, just like Jesus. And you see the world as Jesus did—a place that badly needs truth and love.

TREASURE QUEST

You could describe what you look like by using words such as *girl, tall, black hair,* and *brown eyes*. The Bible uses different kinds of words to describe what it means to look like Jesus— and they're very cool things to be known for. When you look like Jesus, people will be able to spot awesome things in you, like "love, joy, peace, patience, kindness, goodness, faithfulness, gentleness, and self-control" (Galatians 5:22-23).

Shine Like a Star

God promises that you can be a star. Not a movie star or sports star or super-famous singer, but something even more dazzling—a star that stands out like a bright point of light in a world full of darkness and sin. The Bible says this: "You are living with crooked and mean people all around you, among whom you shine like stars in the dark world" (Philippians 2:15 NCV). Living like Jesus makes you different from the people around you. When you start to look like Jesus, you stand out like a star!

Being shiny and bright sounds too hard to be possible. But shining like a star isn't something you do on your own. In fact, there's a way in which you're maybe more like the moon than a star.

After all, stars are gigantic balls of burning gas. They make their own light. But the moon reflects light from the sun, which is the star that lights up our sky. Just like the moon, we are reflectors. We reflect God's light to others. The Bible says we can "reflect the glory of the Lord. And the Lord—who is the Spirit—makes us more and more like him as we are changed into his glorious image" (2 Corinthians 3:18). When you start to look like Jesus, you don't just shine. You shine brighter and brighter!

TRY THIS!

Go out and look at the moon.
Remember that you're just like the moon.
You can't make your own light, but you can
reflect God's light. The sun is millions of
times brighter than the moon.
But the moon still looks awesome—
and it lights up the night!

5
YOU CAN LOOK LIKE JESUS

When You Know God, You Become Like Him

Here's a scene you spot in lots of cartoons and movies: You're strolling through a jungle. You walk into what looks like an ordinary pile of branches and leaves. But you've stepped right into a trap. A rope tightens around your feet. It yanks you upward. Suddenly you're hanging by your ankles!

At first, swinging around upside down might sound like a lot of fun. But when you realize that you're trapped and unable to get free, it won't be so much fun anymore!

Sin's a lot like that. It might feel fun for an instant, but when you realize that you are stuck, it isn't so much fun anymore. It will cause you and others a whole bunch of hurt. And it will tie you up like a prisoner.

Jesus said, "Everyone who sins is a slave of sin" (John 8:34). You can't break free when sin strings you upside down. You can't cut yourself loose or wiggle out. You need someone to rescue you!

God's Big Help

God wants you to know him. He plans for you to become like him and shine like a star. But there's a problem. Lots of times you may try to be good all by yourself. And that's like trying to bust loose when you're all tied up, dangling upside down.

Maybe you've gotten into a bad habit of teasing other kids—and maybe you've tried really hard to fix that awful habit all by yourself.

For example, imagine that you notice that a boy named Shane just got a really bad haircut. You know that you should be nice to him, so you promise yourself that you won't say a single mean word about his goofy hair. You tell yourself over and over to not even glance at Shane's bad haircut. You write yourself notes that remind you to act like Jesus. You try to scare yourself into being good by remembering that teasing gets you into big trouble. But as soon as you see Shane, you burst into giggles. You laugh until your belly hurts!

Can you see it? You're caught in a bad habit and can't break yourself free. It's like there's a rope tied around your ankles and you are swinging upside down. Only God can release you from your bad habit.

Your Number One Job

Here's a secret: You become like God not by trying hard to be good but by knowing God better. When you decide to become like Jesus, your first job isn't to try hard to be a really great person. Your first job is to get to know God.

The Bible says that as you know God better and better, you become more and more like him. It's how you reflect Jesus to everyone around you. It's how you shine like a star.

There's a great Bible passage that explains how this works. It says, "Jesus has the power of God, by which he has given us everything we need to live and to serve God. We have these things because we know him...With these gifts you can share in God's nature, and the world will not ruin you with its evil desires" (2 Peter 1:3-4 NCV).

That's a lot of words, but look at the huge promises the Bible makes.

- Jesus is where you go to get God's power.
- God's power gives you everything you need to become like him.
- You get God's power by knowing him.
- When you have God's power, you break loose from sin!

Knowing God is what makes you look like God. When you know who God is, you start to feel his unending love for you.

See, God knows everything about you, and he could probably find things to tease you about all the time—like when you give a wrong answer in school, when you trip and fall down, or when your own hair looks goofy. But God never makes fun of you. When you experience God's perfect love for you, then you have all the power you need to love other people—even those who don't look very lovable.

The more you know God, the more power you have. It's what happens when you study the Bible to understand who God is and keep thinking about his tremendous love for you. God made you to look like him. He's the only one who can make that happen. Knowing God is the world's most awesome treasure. But becoming like him—that's part of the treasure too!

TREASURE QUEST

Looking like God is a big job, but fortunately, God promises to start right now. Not only that, but he also says that he will keep changing and growing you to look like him up until the very day Christ comes back to earth—the day the job will be done! Look at what Philippians 1:6 says: "I am certain that God, who began the good work within you, will continue his work until it is finally finished on the day when Christ Jesus returns."

6
THE SMARTEST KID ON YOUR BLOCK

God Gives You the Bible
So You Can Enjoy His Protection

icture yourself sailing through the beautiful blue waters of a far-off ocean. You're enjoying the breeze gently tickling your face—until a storm erupts, that is. Powerful winds throw your boat to and fro, and then giant waves toss you overboard! Miraculously, a small raft floats up beside you and you climb on top. You drift through the storm until you land on an island without a single other human being in sight. As you crawl ashore, waves crash, rain beats at your back, and wind blows hard against you.

You're terrified. Yet you spot a cave along the shore. You crawl inside. Even though a wild storm rages outside, you're snug and safe. Not only that, but inside the cave you find a survival manual that explains everything you need to survive on the island. It lists every dangerous thing in your new surroundings—from fierce animals and poisonous plants to big, ugly snakes.

If you were ever stranded all alone on an island, you would be glad to find a book that tells you how to survive. And as you go through life, you will be glad that God gave you his Word, the Bible, to guide you.

Is the Bible Just a Big Fat Rule Book?

If you asked a bunch of kids or adults what the Bible is all about, you would find at least a few who think that the Bible is a big fat rule book.

Well, they're partly right. The Bible is full of history, songs of worship, and yes, rules that tell you what to do—or not to do. But people who say the Bible is just a big list of boring or stupid rules have their thinking goofed up. Through the Bible, God can actually speak to you and guide you through your life. Listen to what the Bible says about itself: "Every Scripture passage is inspired by God. All of them are useful for teaching, pointing out errors, correcting people, and training them for a life that has God's approval. They equip God's servants so that they are completely prepared to do good things" (2 Timothy 3:16-17 GOD'S WORD).

God's Really Good Rules

God's rules teach you to do what is right. And there's a reason for those rules. Listen to this: "This is what the LORD your God wants you to do: Respect the LORD your God, and do what he has told you to do. Love him. Serve the LORD your God with your whole being, and obey the LORD'S commands and laws that I am giving you today for your own good" (Deuteronomy 10:12-13 NCV). Did you catch those last few words? God says loud and clear that he doesn't make rules to ruin your fun. God gives you rules for your own good!

You already know lots of good rules, like "Don't touch a hot stove" or "Look both ways when you cross the street" or "Always let a new dog smell your hand before you pet it." Each of those rules keeps you from getting hurt. God's commands work the same way. His rules protect you. When you follow his rules, it's like finding a peaceful place in the midst of a storm.

God's commands protect you from all kinds of harm. Look at these:

- If you take care of your body, you will be guarded against many dangers and diseases (see 1 Corinthians 6:19-20).

- If you follow God's command to obey to your parents, you will be protected from many bad choices (see Ephesians 6:1-3).

- If you listen to teachers and other people in charge of you, you will stay out of trouble (see Romans 13:3).

The Bible points out all kinds of things that can hurt us—and God's commands tell us how to steer clear of trouble!

Getting Really Smart

Reading and obeying God's commands in the Bible keeps you safe from many problems. It shows you the smart way to live. In fact, learning what the Bible says about how to live can make you the smartest kid on the block. Look at what the Bible says about its proverbs, or wise sayings: "They will teach you how to be wise and self-controlled and will teach you to do what is honest and fair and right. They make the uneducated wise and give knowledge and sense to the young" (Proverbs 1:3-4 NCV).

Almost every time you open your Bible, you will read one or more of God's commands. It's very cool to know that they were written just for you—because God loves you so much that he wants to protect you from hurts both big and small.

TRY THIS!

Next time you read a rule in the Bible that seems dumb or hard to follow, take a few minutes to write down three reasons why you think God gave that command. Get some help from a friend or parent if you need it!

TREASURE QUEST

If you ever wonder whether God's commands are worth obeying, think hard about each of these top ten reasons to follow God's great rules:

1. Sticking close to God is better than anything else (Psalm 84:10).

2. God gives generously to people who do right (Psalm 19:11).

3. God's commands are totally perfect (Psalm 19:7).

4. God's rules make you strong (Psalm 19:7).

5. God's laws make silly people wise (Psalm 19:7).

6. God's commands light your path and keep you from tripping (Psalm 119:105).

7. God's rules are totally fair (Psalm 19:9).

8. God's commands clear up your confusion (Psalm 19:8).

9. God's rules help you understand life (Psalm 19:8).

10. People who trust in God end up happy (Psalm 33:21).

7

GOD'S AWESOME PROMISES

God Gives You the Bible
So You Can Enjoy His Provision

i f you ever washed up on an island all by yourself, you would certainly be overjoyed to find a book that told you how to survive. But you'd need that book to do more than just warn you about staying away from bad stuff like big, hairy spiders. You'd also need for it to tell you how to get all the good stuff you need—like clean water, a warm fire, and something for supper.

So imagine that the book you find also tells you where to find a huge stash of provisions—the kind of food and gear a camper

takes into the wilderness. You'll find a cozy sleeping bag and clothes that are exactly your size, so that you don't have to be cold and soggy. There will be water purifiers so you won't die of thirst. You'll find matches, dry wood, and lots of tasty food so you won't starve. And you'll even find a two-way radio with fresh batteries, so that people can find and rescue you!

That pile of good stuff is like God's care for you. God doesn't stop at protecting you from harm. He also provides everything good you need.

Psalm 23 says that when you follow God along his right paths, he gives you rest in green pastures, leads you beside quiet waters, and renews your strength. Like Psalm 34:10 says, "Those who seek the LORD's help have all the good things they need" (GOD'S WORD).

When you open God's Word, you don't just find rules. You discover all sorts of promises. And you've never seen promises so great! It's exactly what you need to live an exciting life close to God.

God's Great Promises

Check out these examples of God's enormous promises:

- God will give you everything you need. He owns everything in the universe, and he "will supply all your needs from his glorious riches, which have been given to us in Christ Jesus" (Philippians 4:19).

- God will make you strong even when you feel weak. He makes you able to say, "I can do everything through Christ, who gives me strength" (Philippians 4:13).

- God will help you learn to be happy with what you have, whether it's a little or a lot (Philippians 4:11-12).

And then there's the biggest promise of all: God says that he is making a home for you in heaven where you will live with him forever. Jesus said, "There is more than enough room in my Father's home...When everything is ready, I will come and get you, so that you will always be with me where I am" (John 14:2-3).

God's promises are even bigger and better than a pile of provisions on a lonely island. God provides you with everything you need for all of life and for all of eternity!

Don't Miss This!

Here's something really important: God gave you the Bible to protect and provide for you. It tells you all sorts of rules and promises. But it's not enough just to know the truth—or even to

be able to repeat lots of God's Word from memory. You need to act on what you learn!

Your life won't go well if you don't obey your parents. Your body won't stay healthy if you don't stay pure. You won't be happy if you make toys and TVs and other good stuff more important than God. If you want the best of what God offers, you need to obey his Word. The more you obey, the more you experience God's protection and provision!

Back in the Old Testament, Moses reminded God's people that obeying God's Word was totally important. He said, "Take to heart all the words of warning I have given you today. Pass them on as a command to your children so they will obey every word of these instructions. These instructions are not empty words— they are your life!" (Deuteronomy 32:46-47). Got it? Getting into God's Word and obeying what you learn—that's your life!

TREASURE QUEST

In John 10, Jesus explained that he plans a great life for his people. He described himself as a shepherd leading his sheep. He checks them out, one by one, protecting them from harm and providing them with good pasture. And he tell us why he does all of this: "I came so that my sheep will have life and so that they will have everything they need. I am the good shepherd. The good shepherd gives his life for the sheep" (John 10:10-11 GOD'S WORD).

8

HOW TO FIGURE OUT FACTS

Truth Isn't Something You Make Up

He does too!" screams the little kid who just moved in next door. "My dad does too own a truck full of gold!" You snicker and roll your eyes, not believing a word he says. Ever since he came to town a couple weeks ago, your new neighbor has been claiming that his dad has a whole bunch of gold. Not just an itty-bitty pickup truck worth, but a jumbo 18-wheeler full.

You do some quick math and figure out that a load of gold that big is worth about a bazillion dollars. You wonder why a guy

that rich would live in your neighborhood. You want to get to the bottom of the story. "If your dad really has all that gold," you say, "then show me!"

Getting to the bottom of another kid's silly story isn't the only time you want to figure out what's true. When your lunch is missing at school, you want to know who swiped it. When a friend says she just broke the world hula-hooping record, you want to know who saw it. When a coach says that you made the traveling hockey team, you want to know he's not teasing.

Truth is all about finding the facts about what has actually happened. It's about figuring out what's real—and what's not. If you want to find out what's true, you look for evidence. With enough solid evidence, you know what is true.

A Crazy Bad Way to Find Truth

Some people think there's a very different way to decide if something is true. They say that something is true *if you believe it is true.*

That's pretty strange. If you think you own a truck full of gold, you do! If you think you just earned an *A* on your Social Studies test, you did! If you think 2+2=5, it does! If you think eating a dozen donuts each day is good for you, it is! If you think putting on a Superman cape will make you fly, it will!

Of course, when you jump off of your front steps and break your leg, you will soon spot a big problem with this way of thinking. You need *real* truth to get through life.

Here's your chance to learn some big words. *Objective* or *absolute* truth is true no matter who you are or where you live. It's true whether you believe it or not. Christians believe that the Bible is absolutely true. *Subjective* truth is something that's true because you believe it. That's the crazy new way of looking at truth.

Finding Real Truth

Finding the real truth is what matters most of all when it comes to God and the Bible. If you don't have the right facts about God, you could go through life not being sure about who he is or how much he loves you. You wouldn't know how to become like him. And you couldn't be helped by his good rules and great promises. Knowing the truth about God is extremely important!

If you make up your own truth, you miss out on the real truth about God—and that's a very bad thing. You could pray to a god that doesn't exist. You could make awful choices about right and wrong. You might even believe that your poodle is God—until you discover she can't get you into heaven!

Putting the Bible to the Test

You don't want to waste time digging for a treasure that doesn't really exist. You don't want to follow a map that's a fake. If God is the greatest treasure you could ever find, and God's Word is the map that shows the way to that treasure, then you need to know that the Bible is totally true and trustworthy.

The good news is that you can test God's Word to find out if it is true and trustworthy. You can examine the evidence that shows the Bible was written down the way God wanted, and you can see for yourself that the Bible wasn't messed up by the people who copied it for future generations to read.

God wants you to know that his Word is worth trusting. And by checking the facts, you can be sure that the Bible is as great as it claims to be.

9
GOD'S TOTALLY TRUE WORD

You Can Trust God's Word Completely

You would be filled with awe if a bunch of scientists in white lab coats offered you a rocket pack—one of those backpack things that lets you strap in, fly straight up, and zoom through the air like a superhero.

If the rocket pack were real, you could put it on and see the world—or at least a sky-high view of your hometown. When other kids left home early to walk to school, you could sleep in and blast past them at the last minute. Your biggest problem would be picking bugs out of your teeth.

But if the rocket pack didn't work very well, you could be headed for a lot of trouble. Maybe it wouldn't shut off—and it would launch you to the moon. Or maybe it would quit working as you flew around—and send you into a nosedive.

Doing a Safety Check

Before you tried to blast even a few feet off the ground, you would want proof that your rocket pack really worked. You would want to make sure it was safe. You would probably ask one of the scientists to try it first.

That's the kind of confidence you want to have in God's Word. You want to be sure that it will get you where you need to go and that the journey will be safe and fun.

God gave you the Bible so you could know him and become like him. It's how you enjoy his protection and provision. God's Word can do all those great things for you because it is totally true.

Listen to the way King David talked about the greatness of God's Word and all that it does for those who follow it:

> The teachings of the LORD are perfect.
> They renew the soul.
> The testimony of the LORD is dependable.
> It makes gullible people wise.
> The instructions of the LORD are correct.
> They make the heart rejoice.
> The command of the LORD is radiant.
> It makes the eyes shine (Psalm 19:7-8 GOD'S WORD).

David knew that God's Word was perfect, trustworthy, right, and pure. Because the Bible is all those awesome things, reading it makes you strong, wise, happy, and smart. It's not surprising that the Bible is totally true because its author is totally honest. Like Hebrews 6:18 says, "God cannot lie" (GOD'S WORD).

But What If the Bible Is All Wrong?

Christians believe that the Bible is so dependable that they can rely upon it to learn who God is and to find out his great plans. They trust its teachings to help them make life's biggest decisions—like how they should treat others and how they should take care of themselves. They believe the Bible teaches them amazing things.

But what if the book is all wrong? What if it isn't trustworthy? What if the people writing the Bible didn't put down everything God said? What if people made mistakes when they made copies of the Bible? Or what if the stories in the Bible were all made up?

If the Bible isn't true, people couldn't really know God. They wouldn't know the way to heaven. The Bible would be no better than a pretend treasure map pulled from a box of sugarcoated breakfast cereal. The Bible would be as dangerous as a rocket pack that didn't really work.

Putting the Bible to the Test

God gave you the Bible as a treasure map to himself. He designed it to make your life as exciting as strapping into a real-live rocket pack. He wants you to be sure that his Word really tells you about him—to be so confident about his perfect book that you dare to put into action all that it teaches you.

God has given you a book that stands up to the same important questions that you can ask about every other book in the world. You can use the same three truth-tests that scholars use to check the truthfulness of any book:

Test 1: Do the facts inside of the book add up?

Test 2: Was the book passed down without mistakes?

Test 3: Do facts from outside the book back it up?

There is a mountain of evidence that God has watched over the Bible from how it was written to how it was passed down to people for more than 2,000 years. And he gives facts from outside the Bible to back up its claims. The Bible is true through and through, in its details both big and small. Let's look at those facts!

10
THE FACTS OF THE BIBLE ADD UP

God's Word Was Written Down Exactly As God Wanted It

The instant you scored the winning goal in the last seconds of your hometown's championship soccer game, you were famous—at least to everyone within 20 miles. The whole crowd jumped to its feet when the ball zinged past the goalie. But even the kids on the other team were awestruck when the ball punched a hole right through the net.

A few years later, you're telling your story to a kid who has never heard about your game-winning goal. When he doesn't believe you, he's swarmed by a mob of kids who saw your kick with their own eyes. They tell the exact same story that you told.

Fast-forward 60 years. You're sitting in a rocking chair, telling your grandkids about the day you burned a hole in the net. The kids look at you funny, like you're telling a huge fib, and this time

there's no one around to back up your story. Maybe it's true, but maybe it's not.

Then you pull out an old newspaper with a front-page story about your amazing kick—a story written by someone who was there. There's a big picture of you next to the hole you put in the net. Suddenly, your story is easier to believe!

Figuring Out the Facts

The Bible tells an awesome story of God's friendship with the human race. But it's just like when you hear any amazing story. You want to know if the facts are really true.

Lots of old books don't do a good job with facts. Some well-known authors of very old books talk about events that took place many years before they were born—in places they had never visited!

Many books are full of obvious mistakes. That doesn't mean that those writers were trying to lie. But you may have a tough time believing that their words are true.

The facts of a book add up best when two things happen:

1. The facts in the book come from people who actually saw the event.

2. The facts in the book all agree.

These are good tests to use to decide if any book is true, but especially to determine whether a book as important as the Bible is true.

The Bible Was Written by People Who Were There

You might think that God plopped the Bible down on Planet Earth as a fully finished book. Actually, God used human authors to write the Bible little by little. Those authors, however, were careful to write down exactly what God wanted people to know.

The Bible says, "No prophecy ever came from what a person wanted to say, but people led by the Holy Spirit spoke words from God" (2 Peter 1:21 NCV).

Not only that, but the people who wrote the Bible had seen God's actions with their own eyes. For example, the Bible's reports about Jesus come from people who knew him well. They were eyewitnesses to everything he said and did! His friend Peter wrote, "When we apostles told you about the powerful coming of our Lord Jesus Christ, we didn't base our message on clever myths that we made up. Rather, we witnessed his majesty with our own eyes" (2 Peter 1:16 GOD'S WORD).

Everything you learn about Jesus in the Bible was written almost 2,000 years ago, yet the books of the New Testament were written very close to the time that Jesus was alive, while other people who had known him could easily double-check the facts.

The writers of the Bible were so sure of their stories about Jesus that they even dared their enemies to disprove the evidence. Paul once said, "I speak boldly, for I am sure these events are all familiar to [King Agrippa], for they were not done in a corner!" (Acts 26:25-26).

The authors of the Bible might as well have said, "You know these facts are true. I dare you to disprove me!" That's a foolish thing to do if you are spreading lies.

Telling the Same Story

Here's another way that the facts of the Bible add up: The facts all agree! The whole Bible tells the same story. It points people to God, the greatest treasure in the world.

This is especially astounding because the Bible didn't come from the pen of one person trying really hard to make everything fit together. It was written...

- over a 1,500-year span.

- by more than 40 authors.
- by a wide variety of people, including a prince (Moses), a fisherman (Peter), a shepherd (Amos), an army general (Joshua), a king's food-taster (Nehemiah), a prime minister (Daniel), a doctor (Luke), a king (Solomon), and a tax collector (Matthew).
- in places such as the wilderness, in a dungeon, on a hillside, in prison, while traveling, and on an island.
- on three continents: Asia, Africa, and Europe.
- in three languages: Hebrew (used for most of the Old Testament), Aramaic (used for parts of the Old Testament), and Greek (the language of the New Testament). Even though a big mix of people wrote parts of the Bible, the Bible still tells *one message* of how you can know God.

That's amazing! And because all the facts of the Bible add up, you can be sure of the truthfulness of the Bible.

11

PASSED DOWN WITHOUT MISTAKES

God Guarded His Word As It Was Copied

The stories started flying when you stayed home from school for the day. You had the sniffles—just bad enough to curl up for the day in front of the TV. But by morning recess, kids were saying you had strep throat—and a double ear infection. By lunchtime, someone told everyone that you were in the hospital. By the time the last bell rang, they were sure you were never coming back and started selling all the stuff in your desk.

Have you ever noticed how stories change as they pass from person to person? One person tells another...who tells another...who tells another...and soon the story is wildly different!

Even the newest books of the Bible were written almost 2,000 years ago. That was long before computers or e-mail or even printing presses. Nowadays, we can save files on a computer and print out all the perfect copies we want. But back then, a book had to be written by hand. Over time, the ink faded and the books wore out, so new copies had to be made—or the book would be lost forever.

FACTOID

The authors of the Bible didn't type their books on computers. They wrote on materials such as clay tablets, sheepskin, paper made from tall weeds, and calfskin. These books were carefully protected in clay pots, caves, and churches so they would last a long time—hundreds and even thousands of years!

God promised that his Word would last forever. But it seems like this copying and recopying of the Bible could lead to lots of mistakes being made—just like how a story changes over time when it bounces from person to person. A person who copied the books of the Bible might leave out words. Or he might add new ideas.

So you may wonder: Even if the Bible's human authors wrote down exactly what God wanted them to write, how can you be sure that the Bible isn't full of mistakes?

It is important to be sure that the Bible was passed down without mistakes because a messed-up copy of the Bible wouldn't be much of a treasure map. It couldn't tell you for sure what God is like or how you can become like him. You wouldn't know his rules or be sure of his promises.

You can't look back at the actual words written by the authors of the Bible because those very first writings aren't around anymore. But there are two tests you can use to make sure that any old book has been copied without getting messed up. These are:

1. How many copies of the book are there?
2. How much time has passed between when the book was first written and the earliest copy that exists?

The more copies you have of a book—and the older those copies are—the more you can be sure that you are getting the real story.

Checking Out Old Books

Here's a fantastic fact: There are *many* old copies of the Bible—almost 25,000 ancient copies of the New Testament alone! Some are only small pieces of Bible books, but most of these copies contain pieces from all 27 books of the New Testament!

This is truly a sign that God has watched over his Word because there are far more old copies of the Bible than of any other ancient book. For example, there are only 643 early copies of Homer's *Iliad,* a book you might read in school someday. And there are just 10 old copies of Julius Caesar's famous book, *Gallic Wars.*

Even more amazing, the copies that we have of the New Testament are really old. We have pieces of the book of John that are only 50 years older than John's very first copy! We have thousands of copies of the whole New Testament that were made only 200 years after they were written.

That seems like a very long time. But the oldest copies of the *Iliad* are 400 years older than their first writing. And the oldest copies of *Gallic Wars* are more than 700 years older!

Trusting the Old Testament

That's the New Testament. But what about the Old Testament? Well, we know a whole lot about how the books of the Old Testament were copied.

The scribes who copied the Old Testament followed very special rules. Before they started writing, they washed their whole body and put on special clothes. When they began to write the name of God, they couldn't stop until the entire name had been written—even if a king entered the room. They wrote in columns exactly 30 letters wide, putting a space about the size of a thread between every letter. They couldn't copy anything from memory, not even the shortest word. They had to copy everything letter by letter.

When a scribe finished copying a book, he had to count how many times each letter of the alphabet appeared to see if it matched the original. If the new copy had even one mistake, the scribe had to throw it away!

Because we have copies of the Old Testament made over a span of more than 2,000 years, we can check the work of these very special scribes. And they did an incredible job!

A One-of-a-Kind Map

You don't have to wonder if the Bible is a treasure map you can trust. You can depend on the Bible because you know there are more copies of the New Testament than any other ancient book. And we have copies that are truly old! You can also depend on it because you know that the people who copied the Old Testament were incredibly careful to copy those books correctly.

God not only made sure that the Bible was written down just as he wanted, but he also guarded the copying of the Bible. You can be sure that the Bible you hold in your hands today is just the way God wanted it!

12

READING THE ROCKS

God's Word Is Backed Up by Outside Facts

Remember that map to a great treasure buried in your backyard—the one we talked about earlier? You wouldn't think that map was much good if you discovered its directions were all wrong. The map says to walk five paces north from the oak tree, but your yard is full of maples. It says to turn east at the dog house, but you have a cat. It says to dig for the treasure in a certain spot, but all you find is an old hubcap from a car.

There's only one thing you can be sure about with that kind of treasure map: You're going to crumple it up and toss it in the trash.

A Real-Life Map

Some people say that the Bible is as jam-packed with mistakes as a made-up treasure map. They claim it doesn't match known facts from history, geography, or science. But those critics of the Bible have been proven wrong time after time. For example, people said that Moses couldn't have written the first five books of the Bible because writing didn't exist back then—until scholars discovered that writing was invented at least 2,000 years before Moses. People also said that there was no such person as Pontius Pilate, the Roman governor who sentenced Jesus to die on the cross—until archaeologists found writings listing his name.

It's awesome to know that the Bible was written exactly as God wanted and that it was carefully copied for thousands of years. And there's one more reason to believe that the Bible is trustworthy: Facts from outside the Bible say it is. These facts come from two big sources: rocks and writings.

The Stones Shout

Okay, you don't exactly find Bible facts in rocks—but it's a good way to remember that the things archaeologists dig up from the ground often prove that the Bible didn't take place in a land of make-believe. Today you can visit the very real places in which Bible events happened, like Ur, Egypt, Sinai, Babylon, Bethlehem, and Jerusalem. Check out just a little bit of the huge pile of archaeological evidence for the truth of the Bible:

Sodom and Gomorrah. Genesis 19 says that the cities of Sodom and Gomorrah were destroyed by fire and burning sulfur. Excavations at the sites of these cities show that layers of earth were hurled high into the air, causing hot rock to rain down.

Jericho. Joshua 6 says that the Israelites marched around the city of Jericho until its walls fell down. Archaeologists say that the walls fell outward so completely that the attackers could have climbed up and over their ruins into the city, which is exactly what Joshua 6:20 describes.

David. An astonishing clay tablet from nine centuries before Christ talks about both the "House of David" and the "King of

Israel." It proves not only that David was real, but also that he ruled over an important kingdom.

Luke. Much of what we know about the birth of Jesus comes from Luke 2. Luke's facts all check out, such as the Romans having a census every 14 years and making everyone return to his family's home to be counted.

While some puzzles of the Bible remain to be solved, researchers still haven't found any archaeological fact that proves the Bible is wrong. That's amazing!

Reading the Writings

The rocks shout that the facts of the Bible are true. And so do the works of writers living closer to Bible times. These authorities knew all about the events of the New Testament and the claims set forth in Scripture. Three big examples are:

Josephus, who was a famous Jewish historian born just after Christ died. A passage he wrote in AD 93 confirms that Jesus was a real person recognized by many as the Messiah.

Thallus, who wrote in AD 52 that earthquakes and a fearful darkness followed the crucifixion of Christ, just as Luke 23:44-45 describes.

Pliny the Younger, a Roman author, wrote a letter to the Emperor Trajan in about AD 112 talking about many early Christian beliefs. Pliny's letter gives solid evidence that Christians worshipped Jesus as God and followed the practice of eating together as reported in Acts 2:42 and 46.

If you were to pull together everything known about Jesus from ancient non-Christian writings, you would uncover even more facts—including the key facts that Jesus came from Nazareth, lived an extraordinary life, died under Pilate, and was believed to have been raised from the dead. And all of this information comes from *outside* the Bible. This is astonishing stuff! God really wanted to be sure that everything written in his Word was real.

13

UNEARTHING THE TREASURE

Jesus Lives in You Through the Holy Spirit

With your long adventure nearly over, your spine tingles. Together with a group of daring friends, you have hunted buried treasure for countless miles, guided by a prized map across dangling rope bridges, down swirling river rapids, and through dense jungles. Now you have arrived at the precise spot marked on the map. At once, you all tear into the ground with picks and shovels. Soon you hear a loud *clank* as you strike metal. Your eyes grow wide as you lift the lid off of an enormous chest.

Pause for a moment and ponder this: If you were to open that treasure box and find a few hundred dollars, you would be all smiles, and you wouldn't have to think long about how to share or spend that cold cash. Or suppose the box contained keys to a four-wheeler hidden behind a nearby rock. You would instantly know to grab a helmet and go for a ride.

But imagine you were to pry open the box and discover a mysterious thingamabob. You stare and scratch your head. You're not sure what it does. As it blinks, shines, and whirrs, you decide that it's the most stupendous something you have ever seen. There's no doubt about it: That thingamabob is dazzling!

You would have one problem, though. You would need some help figuring out exactly what to do with it!

An Enormous Treasure

Here's some news you have been hearing throughout this book. God is greater than anything you can ever possess, including a made-up thingamabob. He is the best treasure you can ever discover, a find far beyond your wildest imaginations. Yet he's as real as the book you hold in your hands, as near as your next heartbeat, and there's nothing make-believe about this most magnificent of treasures.

Becoming friends with the Lord, however, is a bit like opening a treasure chest and discovering that thingamabob. God is clearly one-of-a-kind awesome, but he is so immense and so dazzling that you will need your whole life on earth just to begin to understand him. In fact, as a Christian, you will spend all of eternity in heaven learning about and living in God's love for you. Yet there will always be more to enjoy!

Understanding the Treasure

God wants so much for you to be his friend that he gave you the Bible to make it possible for you to meet him as your master and enjoy the great life he has planned for you. You can know him and become like him, enjoying his protection and provision. He wants you to live close to him every moment of your life.

God gives you parents and pastors and Sunday school teachers to help you learn all that he wants you to know. But he does something even more amazing than that: God himself teaches you by sending his Holy Spirit to live inside of you. The Bible teaches that the Holy Spirit is God's way of being close to all believers at all times and in all places—including you! Jesus promises, "He lives with you now and later will be in you" (John 14:17).

But there's more.

The Holy Spirit will be a helper to you. He will "teach you everything" (John 14:26). But he won't just fill your mind with facts.

He will also "empower you with inner strength" (Ephesians 3:16). Because you have the Holy Spirit living inside, you not only *can* live close to Jesus, but you also *will* become like him in every way.

God is enormously vast. Learning everything you can about his boundless love for you is a task that never ends. Becoming like him is a job you can't do by yourself. Even if you become an expert at knowing the Bible, cramming your head with commentaries, Bible dictionaries, and other such books, you'll only scratch the surface of God's awesome love. But if you are a believer, you have the Holy Spirit inside you. You have God himself helping you know all there is to know and grow in all the ways there are to grow!

TREASURE QUEST

We all agree that Jesus' followers were incredibly fortunate to learn from the Lord in person. What do you think the disciples' response must have been when Jesus told them he was going to leave them? It's easy to understand why those followers were sad that he was leaving earth and going back to heaven. Yet Jesus said his going was actually good. Once Jesus left, the Holy Spirit could come and be with all believers at once. Because the Holy Spirit is here, God is with you right here and right now—and every moment of every day, no matter where you are.

14

GOD'S HOME IN YOU

The Holy Spirit Is God Living in You

Every kid knows what it's like to feel hurt by another person. Like when you get in a spat with a classmate, and you shout that you won't ever be friends with that person again. Or you wind up sitting alone at lunch or wandering from group to group at recess. Or you play ball with a neighbor, and the game finishes with an inning of pushing and punching. Or maybe someone you love moves away. Or your grandparents wave and head south every winter. Or maybe you get mad at your mom or dad and stomp away.

For all those ways you might feel far from people, you also know plenty of ways to get close. You eat lunch with a friend or dinner with your family. You pack up and go visit your relatives. You pick up the phone, jot a note, shoot off an e-mail, or tweet or text. You can even feel close just thinking about someone.

God himself chose the very best ways to pull close to you because he wants to be close to you. He not only gave you the Bible so you can read all about him, but he also comes in person through the Holy Spirit. And he doesn't just show up for a visit. He lives inside of you.

The Real Spirit

Jesus is closer to you than anything or anyone—so close that you might hear Christians say that he "lives in your heart." That doesn't mean that you have a tiny Jesus camping inside your chest, but that he lives in the very most important part of you. Because you believe in Jesus, his presence inside you is a fact. Like it says in 1 Corinthians 3:16, "Don't you realize that all of you together are the temple of God and that the Spirit of God lives in you?" The Holy Spirit in you makes you an incredibly special place—a temple where God lives. You might say that you and every other Christian are like beautiful little buildings scattered all over the world to show how excellent God is!

It might be hard to understand what the Holy Spirit is like, but here's the big fact to remember. The Holy Spirit is God—along with God the Father and God the Son, Jesus. The Holy Spirit is God without a body. So the Holy Spirit isn't just a feeling, like when you show "spirit" by wearing a school T-shirt or cheering for your favorite team. He is a real person whose job is to be close to you *always,* helping you know all there is to know and grow in all the ways there are to grow.

The Holy Spirit's Inside Job

You can't see the wind, but you can see it sway the trees. You can't see the Holy Spirit, but you can spot all kinds of ways he works inside you. Look at some of the awesome ways you can watch him help you grow:

- He makes you sure that God loves you (Romans 5:5).

- He helps you know Jesus better (Ephesians 3:19).

- He sets you free from sin so that you can choose to obey God (Romans 8:2).

- He teaches you to tell the difference between right and wrong (John 16:8).

- He builds character in you step by step (Galatians 5:22-23).

- He equips you with talents, abilities, and spiritual gifts so you can serve God along with other Christians (1 Corinthians 12:4,11).

When you see these things beginning to happen in you, that's proof that the Holy Spirit is present in your life.

FACTOID

Even though some Bibles call the Holy Spirit the "Holy Ghost," he isn't a ghost like you spot in a cartoon or spooky movie. He's real, and he's alive. He just doesn't have a body, so we can't see him. We say the Spirit is "holy" because he is perfect and pure, just like the Father and the Son.

TREASURE QUEST

Ephesians 5:18-19 is a great verse to memorize and keep in your heart. It says, "Be filled with the Holy Spirit, singing psalms and hymns and spiritual songs among yourselves, and making music to the Lord in your hearts." This passage doesn't mean you should always be bursting out in song, but the Holy Spirit will make your heart glad.

15

LET GOD RULE YOU

Jesus Wants to Be Your Master

Some things in life are tougher than tough. Actually, they're impossible. No matter how much you try...

- you can't ski up a hill—unless it counts to zing down one hill and slide up another.
- you can't bounce to the moon—even if you flap your arms and leap off a picnic table to catch air.
- you can't sleep on the ceiling—because even top bunks always stay firmly planted on the ground.
- you can't dodge spilled milk—it always runs across the table and dribbles onto your lap instead of splashing your chin.
- you can't trip and fall upward—you always go splat on the floor.
- you can't empty a jigsaw puzzle box on a table and expect it to land with all the pieces correctly fitted together.

Anywhere you go on Planet Earth, it's not natural for stuff to soar into the sky and stay there. Because of gravity, everything sooner or later falls to the ground. What goes up must come down—even birds!

It's the same way when we try to follow God's commands. Left to ourselves, we naturally fall into sin. The Bible explains that our sinful selves like to break God's commands. We "want what is against the Spirit" (Galatians 5:17 NCV). As much as we try to do good, it's far easier to do wrong. It's so much easier, in fact, that the Bible declares that "everyone has sinned; we all fall short of God's glorious standard" (Romans 3:23). Our sins include being jealous and envious, making trouble, acting selfishly, living wildly, and even worshipping other gods.

A New Spirit Inside You

God knows that human beings have so much difficulty following his rules that long ago he decided to do something to fix our sin problem. Because we don't naturally obey God, telling us his rules wouldn't be enough. We would need God's help to obey. So he made a plan to change us, making us able to follow him eagerly. Hundreds of years before Jesus was born, God promised us, "I will give you a new heart and put a new spirit in you. I will remove your stubborn hearts and give you obedient hearts. I will put my Spirit in you. I will enable you to live by my laws, and you will obey my rules" (Ezekiel 36:26-27 GOD'S WORD).

The Holy Spirit will go to work inside each Christian to help us understand God's commands and obey them. That's a stunning promise. It's as amazing as if God said he would make human beings able to fly! With the Spirit's help, we don't have to fall into evil.

Your Invitation to Obey God

Here's the catch: The Holy Spirit is at work inside every

Christian, including you and me. But *our* job is to let the Holy Spirit do *his* job. In other words, we rely on him to give us power to live a new and better life of following God's commands.

In the New Testament, the apostle Paul explained this: "Live by following the Spirit. Then you will not do what your sinful selves want" (Galatians 5:16 NCV). Paul also says, "Those who belong to Christ Jesus have crucified their own sinful selves. They have given up their old selfish feelings and the evil things they wanted to do" (Galatians 5:24 NCV). We need to say no to our old sinful ways and yes to the good things the Holy Spirit wants us to do.

Do you want to follow God? If you want to know him better and obey him in every way, the best thing you can do is to tell that to God. You can do so by praying this prayer on your own or with your dad or mom helping you:

> God, thank you for giving me the Bible so I can know you—the greatest treasure. Thank you for sending Jesus to die for my sins, so I can be forgiven by trusting him. God, now I want to know you more. I want to follow you closer and closer. Fill me each day with your Holy Spirit so I have power to obey you. Amen.

That's a mighty prayer that God is sure to answer. The Holy Spirit will work in you to obey God from the heart, with all you think, do, and say—with your all.

Bunches of Good Fruit

When you invite the Holy Spirit to work in you, he helps you follow God's commands in every area of life, from getting along at home to being kind to your friends to working hard at school. You can count on the Holy Spirit to produce good stuff in you as surely as a banana tree makes bananas—awesome things like "love, joy, peace, patience, kindness, goodness, faithfulness, gentleness, and self-control" (Galatians 5:22-23). The Bible calls this the "fruit" of the Holy Spirit. And it's the kind of fruit you can expect to grow when you allow the Holy Spirit to work in you.

TRY THIS!

Plant a small garden in your yard or in a flowerpot. Give the seeds sunshine and water, and let the nutrients in the soil feed your plants so they grow strong. Then think of all the ways that this is a picture of God working in you. When you let the Holy Spirit do his job, growth is as natural and normal as that!

16

LIVE WHAT YOU LEARN

You Can Put the Bible into Action

From the start of this book, you have read that God gave you the Bible so you can know him and become like him. His holy book is a map that launches you on an awesome adventure hunting for the greatest treasure in the whole world—God himself. By reading his Word and being filled with the Holy Spirit, you will grow closer to the Lord every day of your life.

That's not the end of the story or of your adventure. Actually, it's just the start of an exciting eternity living as great friends with God. One day, you and all Christians will live forever with God in heaven. Listen to what it will be like: "God's home is now among his people! He will live with them, and they will be his people. God himself will be with them. He will wipe every tear from their eyes, and there will be no more death or sorrow or crying or pain. All these things are gone forever" (Revelation 21:3-4).

Heaven will be totally fantastic because everyone who lives there will know God and follow his commands. We won't ever act in ways that hurt ourselves or other people. That's why there won't be any sadness in heaven!

Your Head Start on Heaven

As a Christian, you get a head start on heaven right now. Really! By teaching you through his Word and the Holy Spirit, God wants to help you get along with people now the same way we will get along in heaven. He longs to help you love others the same way he loves you, so people will know you belong to God. God wants to teach you how to have the best relationships possible. Page after page of the Bible explains how to...

- Act smart at home. "Children, obey your parents because you belong to the Lord, for this is the right thing to do" (Ephesians 6:1).

- Pick the best friends. "Try hard to live right and to have faith, love, and peace, together with those who trust in the Lord from pure hearts" (2 Timothy 2:22 NCV).

- Respect your teachers and coaches. "For the Lord's sake, yield to the people who have authority in this world" (1 Peter 2:13 NCV).

- Care for the poor. "Religion that God the Father accepts as pure and without fault is this: caring for orphans or widows who need help" (James 1:27 NVC).

- Get along with enemies. "But I say to you, love your enemies. Pray for those who hurt you" (Matthew 5:44 NCV).

- Help people who don't know God. "Always be ready to defend your confidence in God when anyone asks you to explain it. However, make your defense with gentleness and respect" (1 Peter 3:15 GOD'S WORD).

The Bible isn't just about knowing something, but also *doing something with what you know.* That doesn't mean waiting until tomorrow or next week to act on what you learn, but deciding to make a change right now.

Studying Yourself in the Mirror

Picture what you look like first thing in the morning. You stare in the mirror and a kid with messed-up hair stares back. Your breath makes a gross-smelling fog. Fuzz covers your teeth. The front of your pajamas displays a big chocolate blob from the ice cream you ate for a bedtime snack.

When you see yourself all sloppy, you know it's time to scrub up, comb your hair, brush your teeth, and put on clean clothes. Looking in a mirror shows you ways you need to change. It would be really strange if you looked at yourself, walked away, and forgot that you needed to clean up.

The Bible is exactly like looking in a mirror and spotting what you need to straighten up. It would be really strange if you noticed ways you should change but didn't do anything about them! Check out James 1:22-24: "Don't just listen to God's word. You must do what it says. Otherwise, you are only fooling yourselves. For if you listen to the word and don't obey, it is like glancing at your face in a mirror. You see yourself, walk away, and forget what you look like."

Putting the Bible into Action

When you read the Bible, the Holy Spirit helps you see yourself as you really are—all your good points and bad. You see all sorts of ways you need to change—ways you can become more like God.

If you want to keep growing closer to God, you can ask yourself an important question every time you open the Bible to read: "What big job does God have for me right now?"

Here's a simple way to do that. Whenever you read your Bible, have a blank piece of paper handy. At the top of that sheet write *Big Jobs*. Down the left side of the paper, write *My Lord, My Self, My Change,* and *My Prayer*. Leave a couple blank lines between each. Here's the question to ask yourself for each point:

My Lord: What did I learn about God from the passage?

My Self: What did I learn about myself?

My Change: How do I want to act differently?

My Prayer: What do I want to tell God about what I learned?

No matter what Bible passage you read, those four hints will help you act on what you've learned. You'll remember what you learned about God—and about yourself. You'll decide where God wants you to change, and you'll get a chance to ask the Lord for his help.

"Big Jobs" might sound like a lot of work, but it's how reading your Bible gets truly exciting. God gave you his Word to lead you to himself, the world's great treasure. By putting the Bible into practice every day, you grab hold of everything good that God has for you. And that's really cool!

Josh McDowell has been reaching the spiritually skeptical for more than five decades. Since beginning ministry in 1961, Josh has delivered more than 24,000 talks to over 10 million young people in 118 countries. He is the author or coauthor of 120 books, with over 51 million copies distributed worldwide, including *The Unshakable Truth*®, *Evidence for the Historical Jesus*, *More Than a Carpenter* (over 15 million copies printed in 85 languages), and *The New Evidence That Demands a Verdict*, recognized by *World* magazine as one of the 20th century's top 40 books. Josh continues to travel throughout the United States and countries around the world, helping young people and adults strengthen their faith and understanding of Scripture. Josh will tell you that his family is his ministry. He and his wife, Dottie, have been married for over 40 years and have four children and five grandchildren.

Kevin Johnson is the bestselling author and coauthor of more than 50 books and study Bibles for children, youth, and adults, including the popular Deeper series of discipleship studies, *The Peacemaker Student Edition* with Ken Sande, and *The Awesome Book of Bible Answers for Kids* with Josh McDowell. With a background as a youth worker, editor, and teaching pastor, he now leads Emmaus Road Church in metro Minneapolis, where he lives with his wife and three growing children. Learn more at kevinjohnson books.com

THE AWESOME BOOK OF BIBLE ANSWERS FOR KIDS

Kids are curious about Jesus and God and yet, by the time they are teens, the majority stop asking questions about faith and start questioning faith altogether. Respected Christian apologist Josh McDowell and bestselling author Kevin Johnson encourage children to stand on the foundation of truth with this contemporary gathering of concise, welcoming answers for kids ages 8 to 12.

A fun format includes key Bible verses and preteen friendly explorations of topics that matter most to kids:

- God's love and forgiveness
- Right and wrong and making choices
- Jesus, the Holy Spirit, and God's Word
- Different beliefs and religions
- Church, prayer, and sharing faith

The next time a child asks "Who is God?" parents, grandparents, and church leaders will want this practical and engaging volume handy. Helpful tips and conversation ideas for adults will help them connect with kids hungering for straight talk about faith in Jesus.

To learn more about books by Josh McDowell and
Kevin Johnson or to read sample chapters,
log on to our website:

www.harvesthousepublishers.com

HARVEST HOUSE PUBLISHERS

EUGENE, OREGON